"SFK"

Be Blessed by
the words on these
pages!

Love Marguerite

Romans 8:28

From a
MESS
to a
MIRACLE

An Experience of
Forgiveness, Restoration,
and Redemption

Monique A. Brooks

WESTBOW
PRESS®
A DIVISION OF THOMAS NELSON
& ZONDERVAN

This book is a work of non-fiction. Unless otherwise noted, the author
and the publisher make no explicit guarantees as to the accuracy of
the information contained in this book and in some cases, names of
people and places have been altered to protect their privacy.

WestBow Press books may be ordered through booksellers or by contacting:

WestBow Press
A Division of Thomas Nelson & Zondervan
1663 Liberty Drive
Bloomington, IN 47403
www.westbowpress.com
1 (866) 928-1240

Because of the dynamic nature of the Internet, any web addresses or
links contained in this book may have changed since publication and
may no longer be valid. The views expressed in this work are solely those
of the author and do not necessarily reflect the views of the publisher,
and the publisher hereby disclaims any responsibility for them.

Any people depicted in stock imagery provided by Getty Images are
models, and such images are being used for illustrative purposes only.
Certain stock imagery © Getty Images.

Unless marked otherwise, all Scripture quotations are taken from
The ESV® Bible (The Holy Bible, English Standard Version®),
copyright © 2001 by Crossway, a publishing ministry of Good
News Publishers. Used by permission. All rights reserved.

Scripture quotations marked KJV are taken from the King James Version.

ISBN: 978-1-9736-9720-6 (sc)
ISBN: 978-1-9736-9719-0 (hc)
ISBN: 978-1-9736-9771-8 (e)

Library of Congress Control Number: 2020912885

Print information available on the last page.

WestBow Press rev. date: 07/25/2020

If you don't see that your story matters, chances are no one else will either. So even though it isn't always easy, it's important for you to find the strength to share your truth. Because the world needs to hear it.

—Michelle Obama, *Becoming: A Guided Journal for Discovering Your Voice*

Contents

Contents

This book is dedicated to each beauty that reads each word on each page ... for the conviction, the restoration, and the redemption you experience as you read these words. Please allow God to turn your mess into *his* miracle!

A Prayer for My Readers

Abba Father, thank you for giving me the experience and the courage to step out of the boat and into a space of vulnerability in order to share parts of my story, not for my own personal glory but for your glory alone. Thank you for loving me as I am, forgiving my sins, healing my heart, restoring my brokenness and growing me through my mess. God, I pray that for each woman who holds this book in her hands, turning each page with expectancy, you will bring her truths to light. I ask that you place strong faith and resilient courage in her heart so she can share her own story. I pray every woman finds healing, encouragement, and hope in the words written on these pages.

In Jesus' name, Amen.

Forewords

When I consider the contents of *From a Mess to a Miracle*, penned by my first-born daughter, Monique Antoinette Brooks, the word *strength* comes to mind.

Some events in our lives may never be revealed from generation to generation for one reason or another. What strength, vulnerability, courage, and healing it takes to share your most intimate and personal story with all who will read it.

I'm so thankful to God for my daughter and the choice God placed on my heart not to end her life during a time when I knew I had disobeyed His Word and grieved His heart, but to trust Him with the life He had in store for *her*!

God is simply, but intricately, *amazing*!

As I write with tears in my eyes, I don't have enough words to express how very proud I am to be your mom and to see how God is molding you into His woman, with some of the same guilt, shame, trials, difficulties, and victories that many of us face as we grow up in Christ.

I know that your words will be more than a blessing to others as they flow from the pages to hurting hearts and as God touches them with His perfection to convey exactly what He wants to say through you to those who will read them. Your heart is beating fast (as you shared with me) because you're feeling how your transparency has freed you and will free others.

Thank you for the blessed opportunity to be one of the first to share the expressions of your heart!

I love you princess, your mom!

Yes, even your mess can be transformed into a miracle. Even with our poor choices, nothing can keep us from God's redemptive love. We make the mistake of thinking that the messes we create for ourselves are unforgiveable, especially when we don't consult God, but the good news is that if we confess our sins, He is faithful and just to forgive us and cleanse us (1 John 1:9 King James Version).

Monique A. Brooks provides her firsthand account of how appointing ourselves as the decision makers in our lives often results in our making a mess of our lives. But God, who loved us enough to allow his one and only son to die on the cross for us, can transform our mess into miracles that we can't even fathom.

Monique takes us through a journey of hills and valleys in each chapter of the book. Her transparency makes it easy for her readers to see themselves in her accounts. While your mess may not be exactly the same as hers, you'll be able to identify with aspects of her mess that are present in your life, such as spirituality, love, marriage, and self-examination. Her story will encourage you to reflect on your personal experiences as a way to discover areas where you have said *yes* to yourself and *no* to God.

My firsthand experience with God turning the mess of my marriage into a miracle is why this book resonates with me, and it's why I encourage women of all ages to read it.

Ladies, we must know that God has a plan for us, and in spite of our messes he can still restore and redeem us; but we must invite him into our messes in order to see his plans for us come to fruition. Matthew 6:33 (KJV) says, "But seek ye first the kingdom of God and his righteousness; and all these things will be added to you." To see our messes transformed to miracles, we must get the order right—God first, then us. Choose God today by spending time with this vital book penned by my sister and friend, Monique A. Brooks.

—Alisa L. Carson, Trustee, Christian Living Bible teacher,
and deacon's wife at Bayview Church, San Diego

Monique Brooks is the picture of an amazing woman. If you are meeting her for the first time through these pages, I can truly say that being in her presence can almost be an awestruck experience. She is beautiful, smart, and educated, and as you'll find, she has quite a sense of humor. After reading *From a Mess to A Miracle*, I can only stand in awe of God and how he is faithful to deliver us. I am so proud of Monique and her willingness to share her journey with other women. This book is a great guide for women who have ever experienced similar trials and find themselves wondering, "Is there more to life?" This book will help women of all backgrounds discover the truth about love, forgiveness, and surrender and how God can turn any life of mess into a life of miracles!

—Belita D. Butler, owner of Events: Above &
Beyond, director of special events and public
relations at Bayview Church, San Diego

Acknowledgments

To *my* guy, *my* one, *my* husband, *my* friend, *my* pastor, and *so* much more, Terry Wayne Brooks, thank you for accepting me and my mess and for loving all of me. I thank God he led you to find me. You are *my miracle*! I love you with a pragma love!

To our young men, Amarion and Jordan, thank you for loving your momma, protecting your momma and eating whatever your momma cooks! My love for you both runs deeper than you will ever know!

To my queen, my momma, Rhonda D. Beard, thank you for being a beautiful soul and a great example of a godly woman, wife, and mother. Thank you for your sweet but firm corrections, for your encouragement, and for your prayers. Most of all, thank you for choosing my life. Girl, you know I love you with a storge love!

Now for my small but very dynamic team: Donnita Warner (editor and friend), owner of Impressive Edge Writing and Editing Services, thank you for the long hours spent over these words, the laughs, and even the mispronounced words. God brought us together for a different reason but knew our relationship would blossom in this way. You are forever loved and greatly appreciated. Belita Butler, aka B*Boo (PR advisor), owner of Events Above and Beyond, thank you for continuously seeing in me what I sometimes have yet to see. Your support, encouragement, and endless love mean more than you will ever know.

To the wonderful beauties whom I have affectionately named My First Look Team: Rhonda B., Donnita W., Belita B., Alisa C., Sheila H., Shawna C., Lisa D., Rachelle C., Linda L., and Lanee B. J. I appreciate each of you so much for taking the time to be among the first to read the words on these pages, for your invaluable feedback, for going on this journey with me, and for *always* cheering me on. I love each of you with a philia love!

To my WestBow Press Team: Eric- my journey at WestBow Press began with your phone call, thank you for your warm welcome and shared expertise which ultimately allowed me to make the decision to work with WestBow Press. Janine- thank you for being at every juncture of this process. To the Editors, Designers, Marketing and the entire WestBow Press family- thank you for making my first publishing experience one to remember!

To any and everyone who has ever supported me...you know who you are, thank you from the bottom of my heart for always cheering me on and supporting my journey towards becoming a better me!

To my Abba Father, thank you for loving me so much that you decided to turn my mess into a miracle. I am forever grateful to you! It is my prayer that your people are helped to their healing and that you are glorified by the story you have written for not only me but for them as well. I'm thankful for your agape love!

Introduction

Look back on some of the decisions you've made in your life—have you ever strayed far away from doing what is right because what was right may not have aligned with the plans *you* had for your life? Being a divorcee and single mother, I am certainly no different than you. As a matter of fact, unlike some, I was actually raised in the church and conditioned to live a life in line with Christ. Even though I grew up having a relationship with God, I found myself making hasty decisions and plans on my own terms without ever consulting him.

We often do not realize it, but when we choose to do things *our* way and not *God's* way, we are in complete opposition to God and are ultimately guilty of sin. This truth goes as far back as the story of Adam and Eve in the Garden of Eden. God meant for Adam and Eve to live forever, but since they disobeyed him and ate the forbidden fruit, they created an ongoing cycle of sin and death for future generations, to include you and me (Gen. 3:16–22). Now remember, no *one* person can ever undo the sentence given to us by Adam and Eve, but God cared enough about us to do something about that. He decided to show us mercy and allow us access to eternal life in heaven through the sacrifice of Jesus Christ on the cross.

Because of Jesus's sacrifice, no matter how waywardly you have lived your life or how much your mistakes have cost you, God has a plan that can circumvent and positively change any mess you've created in your life. This book is about that change—the change God made in my life following a mess of my own doing.

Whether you made mistakes identical to the ones that I made or have made others, God has a master plan to fix it all. Turning your life over to Christ at any time will immediately start the process. Just as the thief on the cross gave his life to Christ and was given eternal life as he was being crucified alongside Jesus, so can you (Luke 23:40–43). At any age you can accept Christ as your Lord and Savior and live the rest of your life in peace knowing that God has given you a new opportunity to get things right today.

At the end of each chapter are Reflection Questions for your consideration and response. There is also a Prayer Starter; feel free to add to each prayer as the Holy Spirit leads you to do so. My hope is that you read this book with an open heart and an open mind. I trust and pray that as you read, you will be inspired to allow God to take the lead and orchestrate the changes needed in your life to turn your mess into a miracle.

From Prudence to Promiscuity

In the 1950s, *Cinderella* became a fairytale classic for many young girls. It portrayed almost every girl's dream to be a damsel in distress who is rescued by a handsome prince and whisked away to her happily ever after. Today, everywhere you look, you can find the theme of the damsel in distress in many movies, children's books, and even adult books. I guess the question would be, "What lady doesn't want to be rescued?" Does every young lady believe that her existence is not complete without a man coming to rescue her from her humble life? Evidently, this is a supposed fantasy for many women, even today, which is the reason for the continued success of *Cinderella* for the past seventy years.

For me, however, neither Cinderella nor Snow White was my silent mentor. Getting married to Prince Charming and having two children, a dog, and a home surrounded by a white picket fence were none of the aspirations I had for myself. It wasn't because I didn't think I could have those things, but I had other plans. My plans involved building a life for myself by getting an education and having a successful career. I knew that a husband and children would be something that I wanted eventually, but it wasn't something I needed in order to obtain my happily ever after. In my eyes, being a successful, high-powered career woman would give me the satisfaction. So no, the *Cinderella* story and the damsel-in-distress theme didn't match my life plans at all.

Like many career-driven women, I had a blueprint laid out for how my life would go. In this exact order, I would finish college, become a fierce attorney, and later—down the line when my career and finances were booming—I'd get married and have a family. I knew this was how my life was supposed to play out, and I wasn't going to let anyone or anything get in the way of that. Well, that is, until I got to college and, like most college students, those temptations of fun times and extracurricular activities that are not sports affiliated began calling my name.

It was 1998, my second year of college, and up until that point, I had stayed pretty focused on my studies. I was taking accelerated courses, and my schoolwork was bulging at the seams from my core courses and the additional ones I was taking to get me closer to law school. This dedication to reach my career goals lasted all but two semesters of junior college before I became distracted and was thrust into the wild college life of parties, sex, drugs, and alcohol. Every weekend and even some weekdays there were college parties to attend. Football games were the highlight of every Saturday, and the stands would be filled with students who were cramming in schoolwork and studying for tests after a week's worth of partying and procrastinating. The best game of the season was always the annual Gold Coast Classic (natives of San Diego know what I'm talking about), a major event in the city that was attended by many young people, college students, and locals alike. Almost everybody in town came to participate in this yearly extravaganza of partying, football, and even more partying. It was during one of these classics that I met *him*, standing there at the top of the bleachers gazing down at me.

For privacy reasons, I will not disclose his name, so I'll

simply refer to him with a pronoun. That fateful day, I was with a group of friends, and we were making our way up the bleacher stairwell. Once we reached the top to join more friends, I could feel him staring at me like I was the only female who existed in that moment. Who could blame him, though? Back then I was grown (or at least I thought I was), and I knew I was *fine*. I always had my hair laid, the latest kicks, and the cutest outfit. However, I could immediately tell by looking at his outfit that he wasn't from San Diego. He wore a big gold chain, an NBA jersey two sizes bigger than him, slightly baggy pants, and some white Nike Air Force Ones. The fact that he was an outsider kind of captured my attention, which caused me to glance at him a few times as I joked with my friends about whether he was looking at me.

As I continued to have a good time, he and his friends gradually made their way closer and closer to our circle—so close, in fact, that he *accidentally* bumped into me. Acting like I was offended, I quickly snapped my neck around to look at him with the cute "oh no, you didn't" expression. He smiled, apologized, and as planned, eased into some small talk. Hearing his Southern accent confirmed my suspicions that he wasn't from the city. It also made the small attraction I had toward him grow even more. I learned that he had transferred to San Diego as a soldier in the US Army and would be stationed in *my* hometown for the next three years. He told me that he was originally from Beaumont, Texas, which explained the Southern accent. His whole demeanor screamed "country boy!" Being a Cali girl and knowing just about all the brothers in the area, I was fascinated by the idea of having a new male companion who wasn't from here. We continued to talk, and at the end of the night, we exchanged beeper numbers (yep, that was back in the pager-wearing days). Every day after that, we talked on the phone, hung out, and at some point, became inseparable.

Months passed, and we had literally spent every day together. I was head over heels for—this guy. The fact that he was a country boy made him so attractive to me. From the big chains to the baggy clothes and even to his big-bodied car with large rims, tinted windows, and speakers that consumed the entire trunk space, he had me wrapped. I also felt like I had an advantage over the other San Diego girls because I had snagged him before any of them could. I had all of his attention, and he had all of mine. He would come pick me up from my house with a bouquet of flowers and take me to dinner and sometimes to the movies. Now, most women would see flowers and being treated to dates as exciting and sweepingly romantic. However, let's remember that I was a mess back then, and as a result of my being a mess, I found it more exciting when he would come to scoop me up with some weed, we'd go get some alcohol, and then we'd smoke, drink, and have a good time while on a causal drive. *Romantic, right?* Not exactly, but I certainly thought so at the time.

I found it even more attractive that he was a bad boy. You may be wondering, *What made him such a bad boy?* Well, sneaking me into his living space was a no-no, and I found excitement in being snuck in and staying overnight. Something else that made him attractive to me (and this may be a little silly) was the fact that he could cook, which was also not permitted where he lived. His specialty was smothered pork chops, green beans, and rice, all prepared on a hot plate and in a rice cooker in his room. I thought his cooking for me was the sexiest and sweetest thing ever. In my mind we were playing something like house, and as I was looking through love goggles, I began to realize all the plans I had to be a fierce attorney were quickly fading into the background. My complete focus was on him.

During my escapades with this man, I not once consulted God or even asked him, *God, is he the one?* You know why? Because I clearly knew by my actions and knowledge of God's principles that he did not exactly approve of my behavior or this relationship. However, the things that I wanted overshadowed God's disapproval. Oftentimes, when we are thrust into the lust and temptations of the world, we deliberately choose to ignore God's principles because what we want to do feels better than what God wants us to do. This is exactly how I was living my life, being boo'd up with this guy. Everything about him felt good to me, and I did not care what anybody said—he and I were meant to be. Our relationship was officially serious when I took him home to meet my parents. He handled himself so well that they initially approved of him. Now, even though he and I both engaged in unholy extracurricular activities, including sex before marriage, we did manage to attend church together on occasions. Once church was over, however, everything we had heard went out the window, and we were back to smoking, drinking, and well—you get the idea! We continued this lifestyle together for more than two long years before we actually decided to get married.

Reflection

I had my life all planned out from the very beginning. I was on the straight and narrow but allowed the ways of the world to distract me. Peter states in Colossians 3:5, "Put to death therefore what is earthly in you: sexual immorality, impurity, passion, evil desire, and covetousness, which is idolatry." Unfortunately, I allowed the earthly things to take hold of my life. My conformity to the norms of society caused me to completely drift away from my goals and my God.

Similar to me, you may have had plans that you had set in stone. Maybe it was a certain age you wanted to get married, a particular job, or a career that you wanted. However, you may have allowed friends, lovers, and even something such as drugs and alcohol to distract you from that plan. If so, explain your plans and the distractions that you allowed to dissuade you from them.

Prayer Starter: God, help me to seek you first for your plans for my life, and not allow myself or others to have a greater influence. Help me to hear your voice over my desires.

From Promiscuity to Holy Matrimony

The time was rolling around for him to transfer to another duty station. I knew that this day would come eventually, but once it arrived, I knew that I didn't want to be without him. He told me that he had received orders to go to Virginia and would be leaving in less than a month. This was very short notice that the love of my life for the past two and a half years would be gone in a matter of four weeks and I would be left coping with how to function without him. I knew I didn't want to be in a long-distance relationship because those almost never work out. I also knew that I didn't want him going to Virginia and finding another woman who might take my place. Neither did I want to stay in San Diego, where I knew every Tom, Dick, and Harry and would go back to the same old routine. I loved the idea of starting a new life with him in a new place; it all seemed so exciting. Sounds kind of like a fairy-tale, right? Exactly. Ultimately, I laid down my plans of being a career woman and fell for the damsel-in-distress fantasy in hopes that my Prince

Charming would whisk me away from my humble life in San Diego to a whole new world in Virginia.

Realizing my new dreams, he and I had a discussion one day over the phone in which I told him that I didn't want a long-distance relationship. I gave him an ultimatum: either we would get married or we wouldn't be together at all. I hoped that he would agree to marriage, making my fairy tale a reality. And he did. Most women long for a grand and breathtaking proposal, which would have been nice, but due to the time constraints, I settled for a simple agreement. I was so happy and excited about our *discussion* to get married. I knew what I wanted and didn't care about how I went about getting it, just as long as I got it. He never got down on one knee with a ring or did any formal proposal. We unceremoniously went together to pick out our rings, and that was that.

When we shared the news with our parents and my grandparents that we were getting married, they were happy, but of course they had their concerns. My mom and Nana took me to lunch to share with me the sacrifices and challenges of military life and marriage without preparation through counseling. My grandpa, normally a quiet guy, was concerned that I may be pregnant. My fiancé and I reassured our family that we were not pregnant, that we were ready (so we thought) for this major step, and that it was something we definitely wanted to do. However, at the time, I didn't have the slightest clue of how major taking the step toward marriage would be, and I didn't have an inkling of knowledge as to my role as a wife. Above all things, I knew that I loved him, he loved me, and we wanted to be together.

Since my fiancé would be leaving in a matter of a few weeks, time was of the essence. We had to get married before he left or else it would be difficult to arrange a time for a wedding. As a result, we got engaged, planned a wedding, and got married, all in two weeks. It was quick, but I didn't care. I thought that I was ready for marriage, ready to spend the rest of my life with this man, and none of God's red flags nor our family's concerns would stop us. I was so head over heels that I even decided to move forward with marrying him after being disappointed by some of the decisions he had made. Those decisions left me devastated for a while, but again, it didn't stop me from moving forward with the wedding, which is exactly what it ended up being—just a wedding. I'll get more into that.

When it came to choosing the person to officiate our wedding, we assumed my pastor would perform the ceremony. However, he initially refused to marry us because we had not been through his premarital counseling. He even had the nerve to sit me down and tell me that my fiancé was not "the one." *Um, excuse me?* I thought. At that time, I didn't care what anybody believed; he *was* the one, and if my pastor refused to officiate our wedding, we would just find someone else to do it. However, having the big heart that he had and being close to my family since back when my mother was a young adult, he didn't want anyone else to marry us but him. So, he agreed to officiate.

Our wedding day was great. Like most women on their special day, I felt my heart pounding out of my chest from excitement and nervousness while walking down the aisle. My stomach fluttered at the idea that I was going to have the title of *his* wife and he the title of *my* husband. We had our wedding at the church and later had our reception at an off-site venue so that we could have a *really* good time. My wedding day was supposed to be the start of a promising life together, but for the two and a half years leading up to that day, I had grown so out of touch with God, indicating that I was definitely out of touch with reality. It was almost like I was a child daydreaming about all the great possibilities of being married to this man and not even considering the tough times or the hard work it would take to stay married. I didn't even really ponder the fact that I was leaving the only home I'd ever known to relocate from one coast all the way to another. But in fatherly fashion, God was about to slowly reveal to me the mess I had made for myself, and it would take me eight long years to get out.

Reflection

My impatience and desire to take matters into my own hands by rushing into a marriage without ever consulting God is similar to how Abraham's wife, Sarai (who later became Sarah), planned to give her husband a son without God's approval (Genesis 16). Sarah desired a child with Abraham, and God had already promised Abraham a child. The only thing is that God didn't tell Abraham *when* the child would be conceived. As a result of Sarah's impatience with God, she schemed and had her very own husband sleep with her Egyptian servant Hagar in order to conceive a child (Genesis 16:1–4). What we can take from Sarah's actions is that we must understand that God is all-knowing and in total control. He's the only one who knows what's best for us, whether it be our career, our finances, our relationships, or any other aspects of our lives. Since he knows what's best, he also has perfect timing when delivering his blessings. We may see God as taking his sweet time to make things happen in our lives, but it's important to understand that God takes his time to not only prepare us for the greatness he has in store for us but also to protect us from the schemes of the enemy and, mostly, self-sabotage. The only way we can have the abundant life that God has promised us is to consult him in all areas of our lives and then wait on his perfect timing for everything to fall into place.

Have you ever wanted something so badly, whether it be a relationship, a career, or even a child, that you devised a plan to have that something without ever consulting God? If so, describe that specific situation and the steps you took to get it.

What feelings or emotions did you experience at the time you made that decision without God's consultation? Were there feelings of guilt, pleasure, or maybe even instant regret? Please explain.

Prayer Starter: God, I need your help. Please don't allow me to act hastily when making important decisions in my life. It may be difficult at times to hear your voice clearly, but I do desire to move according to your will.

3

From Holy Matrimony to "How Did I Get Here?"

The honeymoon was over, and my new husband and I were now living in Fort Lee, Virginia. I officially felt like a grown-up. It was him and me against the world. We finally had our own place and could do whatever we desired. However, I quickly began to learn that being in a new city where the only person I knew was my husband, who was always off at work, actually put more restrictions on my life than I had when I was back home. Within a few weeks of being in Virginia, I quickly became homesick and husband-sick as well. The first problem was that, when we first moved, the home we stayed in was super old and not what I expected at all. The floors creaked, and there was no bathroom in the master bedroom, which itself was dark and dreary even with light. Simply put, it was uncomfortable. I was disappointed with the little frumpish home we were living in, and I certainly made him aware of my disdain on a regular basis. He constantly tried to reassure me that this was all that was available on base at the time and that we were on the waiting list for a new home, but even with that reassurance there were no guarantees. However, my response to his lack of action resulted in a greater push for us to move off base and into town until we got into the new housing. Rejecting my idea, he didn't want to budge from the current house, and that agitated me even more. Now don't get me wrong: the house wasn't like the one in the movie *The Money Pit*, but it wasn't suitable to my standards either, especially coming from a big, beautiful, modern home in California. It hadn't belonged to me, but it was comfortable nonetheless.

In addition to my issues with the house, I had a problem with the lack of attractions and activities in the city we lived in. Coming from a pretty big tourist city where there were so many fun and interesting things to do and experience, I realized that in Fort Lee, we were literally living in the middle of nowhere. Since I had no clue how to get around by myself, I was forced to stay cooped up in the house all day cooking, cleaning, and reading Zane sex novels, which honestly, were the highlight of my day. The only places I would go alone were the base commissary and the same local restaurants. I felt like getting out and living life to the fullest was no longer within my ability; it was now dependent on when he returned home from work. All of these festering feelings caused me to grow bored of not only Virginia but married life as well.

When I finally got a chance to actually have some freedom and get out of the house to socialize, it would consist of the two of us taking a drive on the weekends to explore the surrounding cities of the DMV (that's D.C., Maryland and Virginia for those not familiar) to hit the club scene with other military couples. While at the clubs, I would have a couple of drinks, dance all night, and in that moment, forget about the issues I grappled with regarding the marriage and the house, both of which I was unhappy with. Our outings would momentarily reignite some of my old feelings for him because I was reminded of the good times we had back in San Diego. Aside from the clubs, we would also get out of the house by going to other military couples' homes to have drinks and chat. Though it was refreshing to finally get out and mingle with other couples on an occasional weekend, I realized that I ultimately missed the freedom I had as a single San Diegan woman. As soon as each Monday rolled around, I was once again stuck. I was faced with the realization that marriage had not freed me, but instead confined me. I began growing miserable and resentful of my decision to marry in the first place. Hesitant to truthfully voice my discontent throughout the first year of our marriage, I took my feelings out on my husband, and we constantly argued over my dissatisfaction and his indifference to make changes. These arguments would be over some of the most trivial things, such as his leaving his dirty clothes on the floor. No way was I going to pipe down. That meant that I would be settling into my unhappiness. I was already doing that, being stuck in the house all week waiting on him to get off. However, he expected me to be okay with the lifestyle we were living and to go with the flow.

In my defense, when I perceived what I considered to be his blatant disregard for my wants and needs, I would attempt to get the upper hand by readily telling him I would leave him and return home to San Diego. In response to my threat, he would run and tell his parents everything we had argued about, causing not only his parents but also mine to get involved in our marriage. We literally were like two kids with no clue of how to handle our own matters cordially. I wasn't about to lie down and do everything he wanted and end up getting the short end of the stick in this marriage. No way—that's not Mo and never has been. However, at that time, I didn't really know what I wanted out of the marriage, nor did I care about what he wanted. As a matter of fact, neither of us knew the true meaning of marriage to begin with. All I knew was that the fairy tale I thought we were supposed to have when he whisked me away to Virginia wasn't a fairy tale at all. There was no white picket fence, no children, and no pets, but I was a damsel in distress. This caused our relationship to suffer.

Our many fights and inability to cohabitate led both of our parents to encourage us to seek counseling to reconcile our differences. Taking their advice, we sought intervention on multiple occasions by going to the base chaplain for marital counseling. Things would momentarily improve, but for me, something was still missing. The feelings that I had for this man when we initially married had faded, and I mean they faded fast. *Is this it?* I often thought. *I've left my family behind to marry this man, and all he does is go to work while I stay in the house waiting for him to get home so that we can argue.* The connection he and I had when we were dating was definitely hanging on by a thread. As I mentioned before, the only way that I would feel somewhat connected to him, like in our premarital days, was when we'd go out to the clubs and have some drinks, which always seemed to be motivation for a good time. My intoxication literally had me stuck in the moment. However, when the next day approached and I sobered up, the party was over and the reality of my resentments came rushing back to me.

Our first year of marriage had passed. We had barely made it through, but we made it. I was devastated by the outcome of that first year, but I didn't try to make things less devastating either. Many women having issues in their marriages would try all they could to make things work with their husbands in hopes of growing a more solid marriage, but I, being the mess that I was, tried to get away from my husband. Because of our tumultuous year and my seething feelings of resentment, I needed a break from him. It was time for me to return home and fulfill the two-week commitment I had previously made to be a returning intern at an annual summer program called Freedom School. *Perfect timing*, I thought. He was totally against my going and even had the audacity to convince his parents to double team me in an attempt to convince me not to go. I can remember it like it was yesterday. They came for a visit, and my husband and I were sitting in their hotel room enjoying their company when, out of the blue, he told them that I wanted to go back home for the program but he didn't want me to go. He laid out all the ridiculous reasons why he thought I should stay, and I sat in that hotel room appalled that he would even bring his parents into it. He cried and complained to them, leading them to gang up on me—at least that's how it felt to me. It was him and his parents against me. They felt the need to go on and on about how it was important for me to stay home with my husband. Now, I loved his parents, but in that moment, I wanted to curse every single one of them out. But I didn't. Instead, I waited until he and I got home, and then I gave him enough curse words for everybody. In the end, I told him I was going back home to fulfill the commitment I had made the year before, and that was that. His actions that day infuriated me to the extent that I became even more desperate to leave him. To get the ball rolling, I called my brother back home and arranged a flight for him to come to Virginia so he could help me drive my car back to San Diego. And that's exactly what we did!

My rebelliousness struck a nerve with my husband, and he called me only to fuss about my stubbornness and threaten to have my car repossessed because he paid all of the bills. Distance definitely did us no good when I left. When he eventually calmed down and would call me to supposedly talk, I would ignore his calls because our conversations always led to an argument about how I should have never left. His actions made it even more clear to me that I wanted out. In order to free myself from the frustration I felt in my marriage, I happily thrust myself back into my old premarital lifestyle once I got to Freedom School. I went to parties, hung out at the clubs, had drinks with friends, got high, and stayed out as late as my body would allow. At this point, my vows meant nothing. I wanted out! I felt so free being away from him, and hanging out with friends made me feel better.

One friend in particular whom I had known since high school was always willing to listen to me when I would vent about my marital problems. Not realizing that two emotionally jacked-up people shouldn't give each other advice, he also confided in me about the issues he was having with his child's mother. One night, a group of us gathered at his place doing what we usually did, laughing the night away as we reminisced about old times. At some point it ended up being the two of us left behind, and we engaged in deep, emotional conversations. We had some drinks, and you know what happens—the alcohol starts speaking and acting. Well, that's when one thing led to another, and it happened: we had a sexual affair. Yes, ladies, I cheated on my husband. I immediately felt guilty. Although I wanted out of my marriage, I knew that what had taken place was wrong. However, it had happened, and there was nothing I could do to make it unhappen. Well, I could have asked God for forgiveness and my husband as well, but remember, I wasn't in the right headspace for all of that. Instead, I balled up my guilt, threw it out the window, and kept my little secret to myself. I decided to resume life as usual, and the guy and I even remained friends after the encounter. Pretty messy, huh? Well, that was me, a big ole' mess. Having grown up in church, knowing God and a little bit of right from wrong, I knew I'd messed up, but that still didn't make me do an about-face from the path I had taken. As the two weeks of my freedom were ending, I contemplated staying home and never going back to my husband. Yet he asked me to return to Fort Lee so that we could work on our marriage. After first refusing, my parents sat me down to encourage me and convince me to go back to Virginia to at least give my marriage another try. So, with great hesitation, a little expectation, and my dirty little secret, I went ahead and decided to return to Virginia to my husband and our marriage.

Reflection

As I'd followed through with my marriage, Sarah followed through and had her servant, Hagar, conceive a child for her husband, Abraham. However, when Sarah realized Hagar was pregnant, she grew jealous of her, which caused Sarah distress and suffering. Like we often blame others, the devil, and even God for our bad circumstances, Sarah blamed Abraham and Hagar for her pain even though she had been the mastermind behind the situation (Genesis 16:4–5).

Ladies, we have to understand that God can see vastly beyond our physical sight. Oftentimes he sends certain people into our lives to confirm his disapproval, but we allow our own desires to overlook those confirmations. God knew the pain it would cause Sarah to have her husband conceive a child with another woman. I mean, who would really be okay with that? Like Sarah, we choose to take matters into our own hands, which often doesn't turn out the way we think it will and ultimately causes us pain and suffering to some degree. In order to avoid this pain and suffering, it is important for us to know that God knows the result of our actions before they even happen. He knows how every decision we make will affect us before we even think about settling on that decision. So, it would behoove us to be patient with God and continuously consult him on our decisions and adhere to the advice of people *he* sends our way to help us navigate the validity and consequences of those decisions.

Was there a time when any of your family or friends tried to forewarn you about the decision you were contemplating? What did they say? Were there any red flags that God revealed to you before you made your decision? How did you respond to those red flags as well as the concerns expressed by family or friends?

What emotions or feelings do you have now in regard to your response or reaction to the warnings that family or friends gave you?

Prayer Starter: God, thank you for looking out for me even when I don't realize it and in spite of the messy situations I create. Please forgive me for my bad choices and for living in opposition of you and what's right.

From "How Did I Get Here?" to Settling In

Some time had passed since I had returned to Virginia, and we had worked things out between us to the extent that I actually began to settle into our life as a married couple. It had been four years since we first moved to Virginia, and to better adjust, as well as keep myself entertained, I began working at the base commissary as a cashier, and my husband and I decided to get a dog. Working at the commissary was fun; it was an opportunity for me to meet some great people from all over the world with whom I could laugh and learn new things.

However, working there was only a small highlight of my day compared to when I got home to our boxer puppy, Slick. Slick was a rescue from the base veterinarian, and he had become my personal sidekick. Now, Slick didn't get his name from the legendary rapper Slick Rick, nor did he get it from the great American jazz drummer Slick Jones. *Our* Slick got his name because that's just how he would act—slick. He would often pull sly moves in defiance of our commands, which would make us crack up in amusement. Sometimes my husband and I would be sitting on the couch watching television, and Slick would try to sneak his way upstairs, which he knew was prohibited without my or my husband's presence. After sternly telling him no, Slick would watch us with that sad puppy-dog face and slowly tiptoe one paw at a time toward the stairs until one paw was resting on the bottom stair. After once again saying no, Slick would quickly bolt up the stairs in opposition. He would also steal our shoes and chew up the toilet tissue in the bathroom, and one time he left a trail of throw up from the laundry room to the front door as a result of digesting Tabasco sauce that he had gotten from the trash can. Though he was disobedient at times, Slick's behaviors caused my husband and me to have more to talk and laugh about, which drew us somewhat closer to each other. It was like Slick was our child. Similar to how parents talk about the new and surprising things their children do, Slick's sneaky antics were always the topic of our conversations. When it was just Slick and me at home, he tagged along with me everywhere. He would nestle next to my feet while I sat on the couch, sit and watch me as I cooked in the kitchen, and even sleep next to my side of the bed during times that my husband was on duty.

With Slick, our marriage was more pleasant and things seemed to be chugging forward. In addition, my career began to advance. I stopped working at the commissary and got another job at a bank as a commercial teller. Having Slick and a job had totally changed my attitude about living in Virginia. In the first year, I had been homesick and miserable because I didn't know anyone or know my way around, and to top it off, I was living in a shaggy old house. However, since then, my husband and I had purchased a new home that I loved, and working full-time gave me a sense of independence and the mental stimulation I needed to survive being away from my hometown. It also provided my husband and me things to talk about other than Slick. With both of us working and having our own priorities, there was a greater sense of bonding between us, resulting in less bickering and more adult conversations. We even slowed down on our extracurricular activities since we both had greater responsibilities. I guess you can say we were growing up together.

To add to our newfound adulthood, we found out that we were expecting a baby. This only added to my sense of family and nesting into our new home in Virginia. It finally felt like things were falling into place. The puppy love and excitement that I had felt for my husband was still long gone, but I actually felt like I could tolerate living with him, especially since we were having a baby. I felt that it would possibly ignite a new sense of love for him. Maybe with a baby, our marriage could actually go the distance. Not only did I notice us having a stronger connection, others had noticed as well. Many of our friends would tell us that they viewed our relationship as strong and happy. This view they had of us would lead them to often ask us for relationship advice, and as if we were marriage experts, we would give it to them. Boy, if they had only known how big of a mess we actually were and that even in the better times of our marriage, he and I were still living outside of God's purpose for our marriage and our roles as husband and wife.

By this time, we had been married for four years, and in all four years I had read my Bible, stepped foot in church, and had alone time with God maybe ten times—not to mention that these few times probably all occurred in the same week. You know, when you go to church on Sunday and the pastor's sermon convicts you to want to do better spiritually, in response, you dive into your Bible for a while, you say your prayers throughout the week, and then shortly after, you've forgotten everything you've learned. Sound familiar? Yeah, I would do just that, knowing good and well I hadn't been raised that way. My husband and I were living on a whim with no sense of biblical foundation to back us up. Of course, my mom and dad would provide that spiritual support, but once I was off the phone with them, I made no real attempt to expand my biblical studies nor devote my time or actions to God. Consequently, since God was not at the center of our union, the breath of fresh air we had gotten from Slick, our careers, and the news of our pregnancy would eventually fade away, once again leaving our marriage struggling for oxygen. Unfortunately, within a few months of finding out about our pregnancy and buying our new home, my husband was up for orders *again*. I was expecting us to transfer somewhere in the States that might be closer to San Diego or even near his family in Texas, but my bubble was quickly burst. When his orders were final, I found myself panicking because I would be starting all over with a new baby on an entirely different side of the world in a place called Daegu, South Korea.

Reflection

Although I grew comfortable with the life my husband and I made, there was still a small voice in the back of my mind whispering, *This isn't it*. I tried my best to ignore this voice because I knew there was truth to it. The truth was that this wasn't it, because God wasn't in it. Knowing this caused me to smother the feelings I had regarding my poor decision to marry when I did. I didn't want to go back home and face the embarrassment that my family and pastor had been right. This fear caused me to feel like I *had* to settle. As I settled, I continued to ignore that little voice and further isolated myself from God. Proverbs 18:1 says, "Whoever isolates himself seeks his own desire; he breaks out against all sound judgment." I sought my own desires when I married my husband without God's approval.

Whether we know it or not, when we leave God out of our life pictures, we are isolating ourselves. However, we must remember that, although we try and isolate ourselves from him, being the good Father that he is, God never leaves us. He always has us within his reach in order to pull us back to him. Most of those pullbacks are unexpected changes to awaken us from our settling slumber, once again giving us the opportunity to turn back to him. That awakening for me happened to be the orders my husband received for Korea. God had to shake things up a bit in my life in order to get me to wake up and reside in a place where I could acknowledge him again.

Have you experienced a wake-up call? If your answer is yes, please describe what God used to get your attention and the feelings and emotions that came with it.

Did you continue to fight, or did you surrender to God? What did you lose or gain as a result of your wake-up call?

Prayer Starter: God, I not only thank you for red flags, but I also thank you for wake-up calls. Help me to be accepting of my wake-up call.

5

From Settling In to a Whole New World

While in my last trimester of pregnancy, my husband and I were in the middle of a big move that would result in our being separated for the first year of his tour in Korea. I would be in San Diego while he'd be in Korea on deployment. I wasn't happy at all with his orders, especially since I had gotten settled in with him and he would miss nearly the entire first year of our child's life. I had expected the arrival of our baby to rekindle those feet-sweeping feelings I had for my husband during our courtship, but since we would be living across the world from each other for the first year, I was no longer sure this would happen. This disruption of the comfy, cozy life I had settled into left me uncertain of what direction our marriage would take.

In fact, even the idea of having to move to the other side of the world after our first year apart frightened me—so much so that the familiar feelings of resentment and returning to San Diego for good came creeping back at times. The fact that we were now having to uproot from my new comfort zone and move to a foreign land had me questioning my commitment to marriage all over again. I thought the idea of living that far away from my family, especially with a baby, was petrifying. How would our baby see our families? Who would help me with the baby? Not that I had given having a baby much thought in the past, but now that it was a reality, I was under the impression that my child would be raised around his or her family. I would picture my mom being there to help me with the baby, guiding me through the milestones of motherhood. Unfortunately, these ideals were quickly dashed by my husband's four-year orders to Korea. He tried to reassure me that everything would be okay and that there would be services available to help us with the baby while in Korea, but his reassurance did little to ease my fears since I was so set on raising our child around family.

Since his orders specified that he would be unaccompanied for the first year, I would be staying at home in San Diego, meaning I had to treasure every moment that the baby and I would have with my family. Thankfully, they would at least be able to be present for the birth and have a whole year watching my son grow. Though being near my family for the baby's arrival brought me great joy and comfort, the move itself brought us a bit of sadness. The realization hit that I would have to give up a beloved part of our family before the move—Slick, my sidekick, couldn't go with us. I would have loved to have Slick around as my baby grew up; however, it began to be too much for me to take care of him during my pregnancy. I was also unable to bring him home to stay with me at my parents' house. Having Slick go to Korea with my husband was also out of the question because he would be deployed as soon as he reported to his new duty station. Knowing that I had to let Slick go broke my heart and only brought greater resentment about having to move. I often thought to myself, *Is this what being a military wife is? Having to let important things and people go without seeing them for an extended period of time?*

Not only was I giving up my puppy, but I also had to give up my job and the wonderful people I had met along the way.

I continued working until a week before our big move, even though I was good and pregnant. I guess you could say that I wanted to hold onto the last scrap of independence and purpose that I felt as a working woman. I knew that once I got back to San Diego and even when I moved to Korea, I would once again be in limbo, not working toward anything, and waiting on the baby to come. This move along with all the hormonal changes that are attached to pregnancy had me on an emotional roller-coaster ride. I went through feelings of sadness, resentment, excitement, and stagnation. While still joyful over eventually becoming a mother, the move and having to start over brought back feelings of discontent. I mean, here I was again, putting my entire life on hold to complement his career.

It had been a week since our move to San Diego, and my husband had stayed two weeks with me prior to reporting to Korea. During that time, we first visited his family in Texas and later stayed at my parents' home in San Diego. Both couples raved over the expectancy of their first grandchild. If I didn't know anything else, I knew this baby would receive a lot of love from both sets of grandparents. My husband and I also shared in their excitement for the arrival of our first child. However, this excitement was bittersweet because he would soon be off to Korea, which meant he would miss the baby's arrival. When the day came for him to leave, I was a little sad. Though I was comfortable in San Diego with my family, I couldn't help but think about some of the memories he and I had made in Virginia. After all, it had been only the two of us for the past four years, and I had finally settled into being married to him. Though we didn't have a great marriage, I had grown comfortable in our relationship and our lifestyle, which still didn't include prayer or church. In all actuality, I may have grown *too* comfortable with him. Instead of actively seeking spiritual, emotional, and mental growth to improve myself and my marriage, I settled into life with him and without *him*—God.

Being back in San Diego and not being able to go out to

the club and partake in some of the extracurricular activities I used to, due to being *very* pregnant, really allowed me time to think about my life and my marriage. I thought about how my dreams of becoming an attorney were dashed, how life was unpredictable due to military transitions, and how ultimately, I may have failed to accomplish anything worth holding onto. My choice to get married had caused me to drift far away from my plans and especially God's plans. With this realization, I decided that while waiting for the baby's arrival, I would reanalyze the path for my life and keep myself busy by taking a few college courses. Happy to once again be working toward my degree, I discovered a new passion that led me to seek a degree in the field of education. I cherished finally being able to function on my own schedule and work toward the goals I had for my life. I still stayed up late at night awaiting my husband's calls since the time difference between California and South Korea was about sixteen hours. When he and I got a chance to communicate, we didn't have much to talk about other than the progress of my pregnancy. Our conversations were short and lacked intimacy. I kind of felt like we were just friends talking and not at all husband and wife. Though our interactions seemed almost platonic, we still said "I love you" to each other, although with not much feeling behind it. It was kind of like I *had* to say it in order for him to not suspect how I really felt about him. The truth was that I literally had no romantic-type longing for him at all. Typically, distance makes the heart grow fonder and women long for their husbands after being away for long periods of time, but for me, I felt like I could go on with or without him, mostly without. Eventually, saying "I love you" became obsolete.

When the baby's delivery day came, I was excited, but once labor began, I was in a lot of pain, mainly in my lower back. However, this pain of childbirth briefly put me in the limelight. The day I was admitted, a film crew from TLC's docuseries *Special Delivery* was at the hospital to capture the deliveries of other expectant moms. Once they got word that I was having a natural childbirth, they asked me if I would consent to their documenting my delivery. Thinking of this as a once-in-a-lifetime opportunity, I consented, and my baby and I got our forty-five minutes of fame, although the actual labor lasted fourteen hours. Even with the various eyes watching me in my most vulnerable state, the delivery went well and our little man came out a good seven pounds even and twenty-one inches long. His delivery was bittersweet because, as we feared, his dad was unable to make it in time for the birth. The original plan was for him to fly in two weeks prior to the baby's due date; however, our son decided to come three weeks early, causing his dad to miss the birth. When he made it to the hospital the next day, I was happy to see him. I was even more happy to see his excitement while holding his son. Nevertheless, those romantic feelings that people usually have when they've birthed a child with the person they are married to still didn't awaken. *What is wrong with me?* I thought. *I'm supposed to be even more in love with this man after experiencing this miracle, right? Maybe it is just the distance,* I thought. *Maybe if I move to Korea things will get better because we'll have the baby to bring us closer, like Slick did.* I lay exhausted in my hospital bed pondering these thoughts while watching him and our son.

Six months had passed since the arrival of our baby boy, and while my husband was back in Korea, I was having a tough time. Even with the help of my parents and grandparents, the reality of being a single mom began to sink in. I was very unhappy, empty, and most of all, exhausted. Here I was with a newborn, still in school, and in a long-distance marriage. The distance between us placed more strain on our relationship than I felt there was before. I knew that if I didn't go to Korea, ultimately things would only get worse between us, resulting in the possible break-up of our family. That would mean that my son could be raised without a father, and I didn't want that to happen. So, once the first year was up, with a bit of hesitation yet a lot of expectation this time, I made the decision to pack up our baby and travel across the water to be with his father. On one hand, I still didn't know what I was stepping into and felt a bit vulnerable without the help of my parents and grandparents. On the other hand, I was excited to be a family and work at rekindling the relationship with my husband—not to mention that the idea of getting an experience of a lifetime living in Korea also seemed exciting.

When my son and I made it into the country, initially, there was a sense of fondness between his father and I since we were now together and had our son as the common denominator. However, within the first year of being there and after settling into a normal little routine, those cozy feelings grew old. I fell back into a bit of a slump, thinking again, *Is this it?* Even the feelings of excitement I had of living in another country had quickly dissipated. Make no mistake, the country was beautiful, the people were very welcoming, and the food and shopping were more enjoyable than Virginia. However, our son was a year old now, and he and I had little outside interactions aside from his dad. The majority of the time, it was the two of us at home while his dad was on duty or even at times deployed. To try to gain more interaction for the both of us, I took a job as a subcontractor for the military as a medical transcriptionist. This position required me to travel to all the military bases near and far within the country, which meant I would be away from home and my baby (or should I say, toddler) for days at a time. Now the tides had turned, and my husband was playing a single dad; he got to experience a little bit of what I had experienced back home. We decided that we would put our son in daycare so he would have an opportunity to interact with other children his age.

Just as in Virginia, I thought that having my own priorities as well as our son would give my husband and me something to talk about, ultimately bringing us closer again. Unfortunately, this time, the more I worked and the more he worked, the further apart we grew. When we were together, there was no spark at all. I had no desire to be intimate with him, nor did I really have the desire to be around him. I guess you can say I grew tired of him. I continued to ask myself, *Why did I come out here? Is there not more to life than this?* Typically, military wives are happy to be near their husbands as often as they can due to the constant deployments. They also tend to find excitement in moving to new places, and for some it's easy to adjust to their new homes. However, over the previous six years, I had had great difficulty adjusting to marriage; then to add being a military wife on top of it was extreme agony for me. I guess after realizing that when I first got married things weren't as I expected them to be and making the decision to settle anyway, I began to grow into a miserable person.

I began to once again question how all the hopes and dreams I had of becoming an attorney or, since being back home, an educator had been wiped away by becoming this man's wife. Now there I was, settling for different jobs in different places because of the hasty decision I had made years earlier to marry him. No longer did my dreams matter. As his wife, I was forced to sit back and watch as he lived out his career. With this revelation growing clearer, I quickly began to realize that my entire marriage was probably a big mistake. If my marriage wasn't a mistake, I reasoned, then I wouldn't continue to feel the recurring resentment and discontent with my husband.

I thought about how the military wives whom I would befriend were "ride or die" for their husbands, no matter where they were relocated or how long their husbands were gone. Why couldn't I feel this way about my husband? Have you ever felt like you were supposed to love someone but couldn't? That was me. Somehow, I couldn't muster up the love for this man. I had felt love before we got married, but was that really love or just lust? Subsequently, I concealed these feelings and continued to act as if I were happy even though I harbored this unfortunate truth. I kept my feelings from him and even my family. When my parents and grandparents called to check on us, I acted as if everything was fine and that our marriage was good. I didn't want my family to know how miserable I was. I thought that telling them the truth would not only cause them to worry about me but, in my mind, lead them to be disappointed in me. What was wrong with me? Why couldn't I just really, truly be happy and be a doting military wife and keep my family together? I thought maybe these feelings would fade as I tried to continue the happy wife façade, but I instead continued living the lie.

Reflection

Once again, I took matters into my own hands without consulting God by going to Korea to be with my husband. I didn't even say a prayer before leaving San Diego, asking God to intervene in our marriage. I packed my bags and left. My rationale for going left me completely unsettled and feeling even worse about my marriage. Now in no way, shape, or form am I telling you ladies that it's okay to leave your marriage when things get tough or when your feelings for your husband tend to fade. Marriage is hard work. Every marriage goes through issues, to include many indifferences and even the loss of love. However, with God at the center, both people know and understand the commitment made and, as active children of God, know that it takes both of them to work together to overcome their marital issues.

Unfortunately, since I had been so far removed from God for seven years of my life, I couldn't figure out a way to get over my negative feelings about my marriage. I didn't pray for my husband, nor did I pray for my marriage to be saved. I knew my husband wasn't spiritually mature enough to pray for our marriage or even for me. With both of us far removed from God, we were going down like a sinking ship with no captain to direct us. Consequently, things only became worse. Psalm 118:8 reads, "It is better to take refuge in the LORD than to trust in man." During this time of trouble, instead of leaning on God and asking him to help me navigate my feelings and comfort me, I kept everything inside. God knew the emotions I was feeling, but he was waiting for me to tell him how I felt, as if it were the first time that he would be hearing it. Instead, I chose to wallow in my negative emotions, which led to my wanting to jump ship from my marriage.

What we must understand is that God is our refuge. He

is the one who can comfort us, heal us, and bring us out of any darkness that we're in. Even if it is self-inflicted or others-inflicted, we need to submit to him and allow him to do his work. The feelings I had about my marriage went through an evolution of great shame, guilt, and ultimately unhappiness. I couldn't tell my family or friends of the unhealthy mental and emotional space I occupied, and since I refused to talk to God about it, I was left feeling alone, lost, and panicked. Let me encourage you to take any problems you have to God. Whether it be loss of love for a husband, thoughts of infidelity, or even feelings of not knowing what you should do in whatever situation you may be in, take it to him. God wants you to tell him. He is open to hear whatever it is you have to say. Know that God can handle your emotions, and in his presence is not a place to suppress them but it's a place to process them. As his daughter, God loves you unconditionally and wants you to live an abundant life.

Have you ever fallen into a dark place as a result of a decision you made that caused you to experience feelings of sadness, loss of love, anger, and maybe even suicide? If so, explain those feelings and what decision and events led to them.

What did you do to navigate the feelings or emotions you experienced? Did you take refuge in God, participate in counseling, and talk to friends, or did you just keep your feelings to yourself?

Prayer Starter: God, when I want to do right, my mind and body cannot, and because of my compulsive and foolish decision-making, I fall into dark spaces.

6

From a Whole New World to My Great Escape

As my misery grew, the more strain there was and the more arguments we had. Like in Virginia, we would argue over the littlest of things. Our good days involved family outings with our son, but when we returned home, he and I couldn't really stand to look at each other. We slept on opposite sides of the bed, and if he attempted to touch me to initiate sex, I would either tell him, "I'm tired," or act as if I was already asleep. Just the idea of having sex with him made me feel somewhat disgusted. It was *that* bad. After a while, I could tell that he was no longer feeling me either. He ultimately stopped trying to initiate sex with me and would go straight to sleep each night. He too seemed as if his heart wasn't into making things work, but just as I was doing, he concealed those feelings and rolled with the punches. Neither one of us put much effort into making our marriage work, but neither one of us made the first move to break it off either.

Our inaction led us to seven years of marriage in which we were simply coexisting, with our child as our only connection. It almost seemed as if we both knew things were drawing to an end, but we were hanging on for the baby's sake. Although we were practically roommates, we never let anyone else suspect how much of a failing marriage we had. Once again, our presentation was so well taken that other couples in his command would come to us for marital and relationship advice. Like the ideal couple, we lent our advice even though we both knew we were living a lie. Yet we were still unable to grasp the concept of God's purpose for marriage and each of our God-given roles and responsibilities as husband and wife. Thinking back, I believe that I didn't want to acknowledge God's reality of marriage. I had ignored my family and my pastor and done exactly what I wanted to do because it felt right at the time. I got married and moved to Virginia because I loved him and wanted to be grown and free, but now, after seven years of marriage, I finally realized that I had made a *big* mistake. As a result, I was stuck far away with a man whom I could barely stand to be around, ultimately feeling trapped—trapped by misery, but also in fear of letting go due to the reality that I had failed the people I loved most and, more than anything, God.

Coming to terms with my feelings, and not being sure of what direction our marriage was headed, I spiraled deeper into misery being in Korea with him to the extent that I was desperate for a way out. After masking my emotions for over a year, I had finally had enough; I could no longer put up a front. Things were over between us, and I couldn't bear living a lie any longer. Suppressing my feelings to portray the perfect couple to avoid exposing the fact that I had failed my family and God had weighed me down. Not only were our living arrangements detrimental to me, but I had to realize that they would ultimately be detrimental to my son. No longer could I hold onto our marriage for the baby's sake. My chance to make my great escape came when my mom called to tell me that she was having surgery within the next month. I explained to my husband how concerned I was for my mother and that I wanted to be present for her surgery and assist her during her healing process. He didn't argue and bought me a ticket with the expectation that I would be coming back shortly after my mom had time to heal. Little did he know, I was not planning on coming back at all.

Reflection

For nearly a decade, from our so-called courtship to the day I walked out on my marriage, I allowed my stubbornness and pride to take over my life. Proverbs 16:18 says, "Pride goes before destruction, and a haughty spirit before a fall." God knew that my stubbornness and pride would lead to my downfall. He even tried to forewarn me on multiple occasions; however, because I refused to listen, he stood by and allowed me to self-destruct.

Having goals and dreams is a beautiful thing, but not including God is what takes away their allure. As I mentioned before, God has a sense of humor. Pride will make you think that you can do life on your own, but God knows how to draw you right back to where you belong. Through my experience, I have found that God uses human frailty to get the glory out of our lives. No matter how off course our lives become, God knows how to order our steps and direct our paths. He stands by and waits for our surrender, but he will never force it upon us. Remember the story of Saul in the New Testament? You may recall that when Jesus knocked Saul off of his horse onto the road to Damascus, he asked him how long he was going to ignore him (Acts 9). Before Saul was renamed Paul, he was forewarned that he was on the wrong path. God had let him live his own way for a good length of time, but God's plans took over Saul's life and his ways of destruction.

Although God doesn't force our surrender to him, he will shift our lives to a point where surrender is necessary. I had reached my point of self-destruction to the extent that I had no other choice but to return home to get back to God. We must remember that God is speaking all the time, but the reason it's so difficult for us to hear him is that we allow our plans to scream louder. We must learn to silence the hustle and bustle of our fleshly desires in order to hear the instructions God is trying to give us. If we don't, we are at risk for self-sabotage and open to the schemes of the enemy. However, even if we've reached rock bottom, God can still take our hard hearts and make them supple so that he can place his will in them. Remember, ladies, surrendering to God takes away the sting of our personal plans going awry.

Piggybacking off of the chapter 5 reflection, how did you eventually escape from the dark place you were in caused by the decision you made? Explain the events that led to your freedom.

Did you believe at the time or do you believe even today that the events that led to your escape were a shift of God's doing? Explain how you do or do not believe God bailed you out.

Monique A. Brooks

Prayer Starter: God, thank you for looking beyond our shortcomings and coming to our rescue.

7

From My Great Escape to My Hidden Darkness

When the time came for me to leave, I had already put in my two-week notice with my job and packed up me and my son's clothes. When I got to San Diego, I felt a sense of great relief but also great shame. My family still didn't know that I was leaving my husband for good, but I knew when the question arose of when I would be returning to Korea that I would eventually have to face the music and tell them the truth. I felt that the right time to tell them would be after my mom had healed from her surgery. Though my family didn't know about my permanent departure, I did eventually reveal my intentions of leaving for good to my husband.

During one of our few phone conversations, I admitted to him that I could no longer live how we were living and I simply wasn't happy in our marriage. With hesitation to end things, he ultimately concurred that things were not the same between us and that he had grown unhappy as well. Subsequently, just as we had made an agreement over the phone to get married, we also made an agreement over the phone to get divorced. In spite of things having ended like I desired, the fact that we were getting a divorce still brought me more pain than pleasure. I had drifted from God's Word for nine years, but the one thing I did remember is that God hates divorce.

Knowing that my divorce was of my own doing from the very beginning made me feel as if I had betrayed God. The guilt of my betrayal only deepened once I told my family that my husband and I had ended things. They had their questions as to why, but I could only tell them that I didn't love him anymore. There was nothing I could do to get those feelings back that I had in our first two years of dating. Though he also had made his fair share of mistakes in our marriage, I felt that I was to blame for its ending. My lack of preparation for marriage caused me to miss God's purpose for it. Missing God's purpose for marriage and for my role as a wife made it difficult for me to cope with the transitions and the many ups and downs that come with married life. My lack of coping skills caused me to ultimately be miserable and my love for my husband to burn out. Even though I felt as if I had betrayed everyone by my rebelliousness seven years earlier, my family had never treated me as if I were to blame. They never even said, "We told you so." They were very supportive throughout my entire life transition.

Nevertheless, my own personal guilt trips that I placed on myself left me dealing with some major emotional demons. Being back home and having to be the showcase of a marriage that I know people questioned from the jump made me feel like a fool. Not only had I not listened to God, but I also hadn't listened to the people God had placed in my path to help redirect me from my own actions. I, being raised in a God-fearing family, had grown up knowing what it meant to live for God and knew now that I had ultimately failed at doing so. How humiliating is that? Have you ever felt humiliated and realized you were the cause of your humiliation? I certainly have, and it felt *horrible*.

This feeling of failure brought me much grief to the extent that I often found myself sitting in the closet of my room crying uncontrollably. Consequently, I was still embarrassed to turn my face to God and ask for help, which left me feeling alone and helpless. Why should I ask for help? I felt so undeserving of his help. I had deliberately lived without seeking his help for the last seven years, so why should I go running back screaming "Abba, Father" now? Would he even desire to help me after how blatantly disobedient I was?

In addition to my crying spells, I would often find myself laughing hysterically when spending time with my family, but that laugh would produce tears that quickly grew into a concealed cry for help. Everyone assumed I was crying in laughter along with the group. However, my crying was so inconspicuous that no one actually knew that I was an emotional wreck—well, everyone except for my mother, that is. She began noticing how I would often have to excuse myself from the room at family gatherings to "use the bathroom," just after being asked by a relative when I would be going back to Korea. These bathroom runs were actually cry breaks. I would go into the bathroom flustered over having to answer that I was back home and staying with my parents because my marriage had failed. I was in fear of family members asking deeper questions about the break-up, such as how I would be raising my son without his father. I was also in fear of them possibly trying to convince me to make things work when I knew things were definitely over.

I tried to hide my feelings from the world through my laugh-cry and my bathroom breaks, but my mom, being as in tune with me as she is, was onto me. She would often ask me when I was quiet and alone whether or not I was depressed. At first, I denied it and continued to put on a front, but after some time with no improvement in my emotional state, I started to question myself: *Am I really depressed?* The answer was *yes!* This divorce was taking a greater toll on me than I ever realized. I was in such a dark place that my entire lifestyle changed. During my depression, I lost over twenty pounds due to my lack of appetite, and as a result, I began to appear malnourished.

I had bags under my eyes, and my face appeared sunken in. I stopped hanging out with my longtime friends and attended the early church service to avoid the whispers and questions from the other young adults and the family friends I knew well. I avoided engaging in conversation with anyone for fear they'd ask me, 'How's your husband?" "Where's your ring?" As you all know, church folk can be bold, especially the ones who don't have your best interest at heart. Knowing this, I wanted to avoid everyone. When I sat in the sanctuary, in a room full of people, I felt completely alone. When I had my son with me and we would walk to and from the car at church, I felt that he and I were under everyone's microscope.

Although the divorce wasn't final, it literally felt like I was walking around with a big sign on my shirt that said, "Divorced, Single Mom." In my mind, everyone knew the various issues that come along with divorce, and everyone at church knew that if you got a divorce, it's a major failure of your commitment to not only your husband but mainly to God. Now everyone knew that I, Monique, a child of God, had failed him. My constant concern over the entire church frowning upon my betrayal of God was only a figment of my own imagination. Unfortunately, I didn't realize that I was paranoid because that's just how guilt and humiliation manipulate your thoughts.

Reflection

Although I had escaped the prison I was in, I was now tasked with facing the hard truth of my poor decisions. Oftentimes we believe that when we escape a miserable situation, we are supposed to come out free and happy on the other side. Though this may be true in some cases, in most cases it's not. When we decide to sit and face the hard truth of our disobedience toward God and the pain it has caused us, it can leave us feeling vulnerable from the heat or consequences we must face as a result of our own actions. I like to think of this time after my escape as a time of tempering. Tempering is a method of placing metal under extreme heat, causing it to be less hardened. Steel can withstand temperatures as hot as 1,112 degrees Fahrenheit. Pretty hot, right? During the heating process, the steel turns many different colors, including straw yellow, orange, purple, blue, and even light blue. In the end, the steel is tougher and better prepared for use, which was the ultimate purpose of it being heated in the first place. Similar to tempering, God allowed me to go through the heat in which I became vulnerable, having experienced various emotions, or colors, all the way down to deep depression. God was not only taking me through the tempering process to soften me and leave me weak but he also had me under the fire in order to build my spiritual strength. Once my exterior was unhardened and I was left vulnerable, I was open to letting God back in. In 1 Peter 5:10, we read, "After you have suffered a little while, the God of all grace, who has called you to his eternal glory in Christ, will himself restore, confirm, strengthen, and establish you." We will all have times when we are suffering from the heat; however, we must remember that our suffering is not in vain and God is only using this process to make us stronger. I was on my way to experiencing my restoration, my confirmation, and my strengthening that would eventually lead me to my establishment.

What happened after you escaped from your dark situation? Was the grass greener on the other side, or did you have to go through the tempering process first? Please explain.

During your tempering process, what were the feelings and thoughts you experienced? Who did you lean on during this time of tempering? God? A friend or family member? How did he or they help you through this process?

Prayer Starter: God, please give me the courage to accept my tempering process and the strength to endure the heat while in the process.

From My Hidden Darkness to Forgiveness and Healing

After months of feeling shame and guilt, one Sunday came along that I remember clearly. It was the turning point for those feelings to change. As I sat in church listening to my pastor share his sermon, I suddenly felt an overwhelming feeling of reassurance that, after everything I was going through, I was going to be okay. That little voice in the back of my mind was speaking again, but this time it was saying, *It's okay, Mo. It's going to be okay.* Maybe it was the Holy Spirit speaking to me, but that day, I walked out of church with a sense of peace— the kind of peace that helped me to gradually stop beating myself up over the circumstances I had caused. I slowly began turning my face to God outside of attending church and really began spending intimate time with him. I would read his Word, express my feelings to him, and ask for forgiveness, strength, and healing to get me through my transition. Sure enough, with each passing day, things seemed brighter.

I gradually began coming out of my cave of affliction and started to regain my confidence. I slowly started involving myself in ministry. This led to my reconnection with my church family. Their warm nature relieved my fears of ridicule from others. Being at home and surrounded by family who live their lives on the foundation of God's Word really helped me rekindle my relationship with God. During my reconnection with Christ, I began to learn through his Word and the reassurance of my family how deeply God's forgiveness flows. This realization allowed me to open up to God about my sins, which led to my confession and then my asking for his forgiveness. During this period, I learned that no one is owed forgiveness, but as God's children, God grants it to us when we ask for it. There's such a refreshing, cleansing, and freeing feeling that comes with knowing you've been forgiven. Forgiveness is such a precious gift—who wouldn't want to experience it? After all, God gives it *abundantly*. When forgiving myself, I had to realize that since God's forgiveness flows abundantly and he doesn't hold me in contempt for my disobedience, there's no valid reason for me to hold myself in contempt. Romans 3:23 says, "For all have sinned and fall short of the glory of God." This truth of God's Word provided me with great peace.

Before I even knew I was going to disobey God by my actions, God already had the jump on me. However, he didn't hold my self-inflicted mess against me. Just thinking of how I participated in promiscuity, drunkenness, and even adultery made me realize how much of a mess I really had been. For all these mistakes and the thousands more that I made, God's provision for those mistakes is Jesus. Jesus came to the earth and died on the cross just for situations like mine. Because of his great sacrifice, I am no longer living under condemnation of my sins. This does not, however, give me a pass to continue doing wrong after I have been made free, but it gives me spiritual maturity to know that, with the power of the great Comforter, I can be forgiven for my sins and have been granted mercy and opportunities to do better. My spiritual growth during my healing was manifested only through my acknowledgement of how much of a mess I had become and laying that mess at the feet of God in surrender to Him. My duty after giving my mess to God was to never return to it; that's true repentance. My desire during my college years and married life was only to please myself, but after my decisions left me sitting in a divorce and in despair, my desire was redirected toward wanting only to please God.

I had been lost in a self-created muck, yet God had never rejected me. In Deuteronomy 31:6, it says, "Be strong and courageous. Do not fear or be in dread of them, for it is the LORD your God who goes with you. He will never leave you or forsake you." These words are such an encouraging promise. I took them and turned my loneliness into solitude, which led to my reconnection to God. Although still alone, I was no longer depressed or lonely because I was in his presence. Life looked better than it ever had. It made me understand that there is nothing that can separate me from the love of my Savior. He had been there all the time waiting for me to surrender to him. I had created a mess, but God was waiting to perform his miracle.

My willingness to let go and confess my sins to God was a major turning point in my life. It allotted me forgiveness, and forgiveness lifts burdens. Many dilemmas in life can be solved with forgiveness. Unfortunately, I believe that it is a hard concept for most people, including me, to practice or experience. Forgiveness is not a reward for good behavior, nor is it a prize to the most gifted. It is an inexplicable gift designed by God that gives the giver and receiver undeserved peace. There is a freedom from hurt and pain that can be accomplished only through forgiveness. The reason many find it so hard to practice, I believe, is that it cannot be deciphered by the intellect, emotions, or any other human means. The awesome power of forgiveness is so phenomenally described because it is what God did for each of us when he sent his only Son to die on a cross for our sins. He was a perfect sacrifice. This means that he had done no wrong, yet he suffered for the wrongs of all humans. The same authority God used to send his Son, Jesus, to die for our sins is the same authority God gives to us to extend forgiveness to others. But the problem is that most people will not use what they do not understand. Forgiveness will forever remain a dilemma, but it can be a dominant force in our lives if we make great effort to apply it.

Reflection

Whether you disobey God or others offend you, forgiveness is part of the package of God's grace given to a lost world. Grace is God's unmerited favor, meaning you can do nothing to deserve it. My strength to forgive others comes from my recollection of how God has forgiven me for all the wrong I have done. Even more important than this is that, when I compare the pain and disappointment I've experienced as a victim to the pain and disappointments and extreme displeasures and grievances I have brought against God, *there is absolutely no comparison!* In light of all of this, God is still faithful to forgive. There is only one small requirement that God asks of us: "If we confess our sins" (1 John 1:9), the Word says God will forgive us. We have a responsibility to confess our sins because God cannot heal what we do not reveal.

The decision to rededicate my life to God was a private one. It was between me and my Savior. I did not want a spectacle; I didn't walk down the aisle or even talk to the pastor about it. I made a sincere decision that from that Sunday when he reassured me of his presence in my life, my goal moving forward was to do better. One of the biggest obstacles was my concern about what others would think about my divorce, but God even took that feeling away from me. Psalm 34:18–19 says, "The LORD is near to the brokenhearted; He saves the crushed in spirit. Many are the afflictions of the righteous, but the LORD delivers him from them all." The Lord knew the pain I was going through, and after allowing me to suffer a while, he reassured me that he was there to pick me up. I no longer worried about what others thought. When those around me eventually found out about my divorce, they were distraught, but I had a peace that I could not begin to understand or explain. God had taken away the pain. I realized that all God ever wanted was my heart. When I gave it to him, all else really didn't matter. My private decision to surrender to God turned into my public joy.

After coming out of your dark place, did you ask God for forgiveness for the decisions you had made that went against Him? If so, how did you feel after you confessed to God? Did things turn around for you?

If you didn't ask God for forgiveness, there's no better time than now. Take a few minutes to think about your sins against him that led you to your dark place. Write those sins down and ask God for his forgiveness. Remember, there is no right or wrong way to confess and ask God for forgiveness. All you have to do is be as open as you would be with your best friend. Just remember, he is your father, and he wants to hear what you have to say.

Prayer Starter: God, thank you for your faithfulness to me. Thank you for your forgiveness extended to me, and thank you for healing my wounded places.

9

From Forgiveness and Healing to Restoration

After realizing that God had forgiven me for my sins and then forgiving myself, my life began turning in a positive direction. I enrolled in school and was close to beginning my internship. I was serving as the youth choir director and leading Bible study classes. I grew excited in the moments that I could spend with God. It brought me great joy to reflect on what he had done for me, the transformation he was taking me through, and thank him for my many blessings. Praying to God also brought me great relief from the anxiety, loneliness, and sadness I experienced. Spending time with God during prayer and studying his Word made life much better. My home life was great; my son was a happy, active, three-year old; and my family couldn't be any more supportive of me through all my transitions. While the divorce was yet to be final, my ex and I stayed cordial, and he would call at least once a week to talk to our son. Over time, the calls grew more distant between one call to the next. Eventually, my son heard from his father only about once every few months, and then it was not through a phone call but an email that he sent to me. Even when he wasn't deployed and transferred to a state closer to California, the visits were few and so were the phone calls.

Nevertheless, I didn't allow the absence of his father to drag me back into feelings of guilt or frustration. Though his dad wasn't always there, my son was well taken care of and had great male role models in my dad, granddad, and his godfather. My focus was on moving forward and providing a better life for me and my son, except this time, it would be on God's terms. This restoration phase of my life really propelled my spiritual, mental, and emotional growth. It even enhanced my physical growth, enabling me to get back to a healthy weight and appearance. I stopped walking with my head down in humiliation and began walking with a confidence that only God can provide. I was confident in his love, and what others said or thought was no longer a factor. Eventually, I began sticking around after church to talk to other church members with genuine delight. With my mom's encouragement, I made the effort to reconnect with a few friends, which would allow me the opportunity to take mommy breaks and occasionally have *responsible* nights out with the ladies. This was refreshing, especially after a week full of school, church, and being on twenty-four-seven mommy duty. God was restoring and reviving me, and it felt *so* good. Now, by no means am I saying that I was a saint, but I was thankful for God's love and willingness to grant me grace and mercy and help me turn my life in the right direction.

Initially, I harbored a fear of returning home after my divorce and fully taking on the role as a single mother. Nonetheless, God eliminated those fears and proved to me that I could do it if I just leaned on him for strength. I learned that God's love for me was so great that he was willing to give me another chance to get things right. I was looking forward to the plans God had for my life, and more than anything I was ready and willing to follow them. I knew that if God could forgive me and grant me a newfound worth and confidence after almost eight years of bad decision making, he would definitely grant me a second chance at providing a greater life for me and my son.

Even though I had turned my focus to God and was navigating through his direction for my life, there were still times when the enemy would try to distract me by attempting to hang a dark cloud over my head to remind me that the divorce still wasn't final. During these moments I would become a bit weary in my waiting, but with my new focus and relationship with God, I would pray and give these worries to him. Little did I know; my heavenly Father gathered my prayers and was working behind the scenes to develop a plan that would put the devil in his place. God is constantly strategizing, and he tends to place certain people in our paths to help us through our waiting. To my surprise, God would soon send a special friend to help me do just that.

It was a Sunday in 2007, and church had concluded. Several people were lingering in the parking lot chatting in different circles while a sister-friend of mine and I were at our cars talking. During our conversation, I became concerned when I no longer had eyes on my son, who at some point had run off from where we were. I didn't worry too much because everyone at church knew whom he belonged to, especially since we all looked after each other's children. As I made my way through the church parking lot, I noticed a group of people gathered around a cream-colored Chrysler 300 that was booming loud gospel music. After examining the crowd for my son, I suddenly saw a little brown head crowning barely above the window of the passenger seat of the car. I quickly stormed over to the car and saw my child sitting next to a male driver whom I didn't know. Slightly embarrassed, I opened the passenger door to the man's car and grabbed my son. The man, while still sitting in the driver seat, tried to reassure me that it was okay for him to be in his car, but I didn't want to hear that. I didn't even know this dude. I grabbed my boy by the arm and briskly walked over to my car in a bit of frustration and, as I mentioned before, slight embarrassment. I wanted to scold him, but he was only three and probably assumed that everyone at church was safe to be around. As I buckled him into his car seat, my sister-friend and I continued our conversation, at which time the man with the Chrysler 300 walked over to us and decided to chime in. He asked us if we liked Chicago gospel music, and we replied that we hadn't really heard it before. He then said that he had some CDs he could give us so we could take a listen. I was thinking, *Who is this dude? Is he a musician or bootleg CD man?* He introduced himself as Terry Brooks. Cordially, we shared our names with him in return. After talking to him a few minutes longer, he casually walked back to his car. After the encounter, I went home that day thinking nothing more of this guy or his CDs.

A few weeks had passed since that encounter in the church parking lot when, to my surprise, I received an e-mail through my MySpace account from a Terry Brooks. My initial thought was, *Now I know this isn't that same Terry Brooks from the parking lot?* I continued to read his message, and sure enough, it was him! I couldn't believe it—this man had found me on social media. His message referred to the parking lot conversation about the music he wanted to share, or at least that's what he said. He found out I was the youth choir director and asked if he could stop by rehearsal to drop off the CDs. I welcomed his visit, and we made the arrangements to meet. When he came, we briefly spoke, he gave me the music, and he was on his way. After listening to the music he shared with me and being pleased by what I heard, I selected a few songs to teach the youth choir for future Sundays. I then messaged him back on MySpace to thank him for sharing the music. This message sparked an ongoing dialogue between the two of us that eventually led to the exchange of phone numbers. As the youth choir director, I had developed a love for all genres of gospel music, and this guy had a knack and intellect for it that greatly intrigued me. Our identical passion for music would be the bridge that connected us, and that's where our friendship began. On top of our shared interest in music, we each had the responsibility of being parents, single parents at that. He had a son who was six years older than mine.

Time passed, and our conversations not only continued but grew deeper in content. We learned there was another commonality we shared—the life-altering experience called divorce. Neither of us were proud of the circumstances; however, life happens, and at the time we were both in the final stages of our divorce proceedings. Listen, God certainly has a sense of humor! By this time, our friendship was tight, but it was only that—a tight friendship. Because we had grown so close, we found comfort in each other during this painful experience that we both shared privately. The mutual support and interests we shared allowed us to grow even closer. I didn't see it at the time but later realized that God was restoring us as we would encourage each other to push through despite the current circumstances, and believe me, there were some days that were pretty ugly. I was extremely grateful for this friendship, one with someone of the opposite sex and with no strings attached. I went about this relationship differently and acknowledged that I could have a male friend and it be just that. God began to reveal to me that 2007 would prove to be a turning point in my life toward the direction he was guiding me.

Reflection

To be better, I needed to do things differently. All of us are creatures of habit, and if we do not pay attention to what we do, it can become natural to repeat things that do not turn out well. I was determined that this was not going to happen to me. Making better choices was now a priority. Proverbs 3:6 says that we should acknowledge God in all that we do and he will show us which way to go. There is a certainty in seeking direction from God, and that is through direct prayer to Him. Prayer is not only a requirement for building an intimate relationship with God, it is also a necessity. Recommitting my life to him was only the beginning.

"The Lord is near to all who call on him, to all who call on him in truth" (Psalm 145:18). Duplicating the exact prayers I heard growing up is not what God was expecting of me. He had given me my own story, and he wanted me to have my own conversation with him. What he wants is sincerity, and my desire was to be just that—sincere. Prayer took on a whole new meaning for me. It was very personal, and it allowed me to make a real connection. I knew that the Lord heard me and I was not ashamed to share everything with him. He listened as I spoke to him in truth. As a result, he brought someone into my life who would lead me closer to him and help me remove the trap in which the enemy was still trying to capture me.

From reading about my situation, what can you do to draw nearer to God? What steps can you take to better learn who he is and the direction he has for your life?

Has God ever brought someone into your life who helped you be a better you? Who is this person, and what did he or she do to help you?

Prayer Starter: Thank you God for being available to hear my prayers and for sending people into my life to help me grow closer to you during my journey through restoration.

**Special Assignment: After you take a moment to thank God for sending people your way, go a step further and personally reach out to them and thank them for being *those* people God sent specifically for you.

10

From Restoration to Redemption

When my divorce became final, I began to struggle on some days while dealing with my son's father. Certain loose ends between us regarding the divorce left me frustrated. However, Terry knew just what to say to help me through these difficult times. I was so grateful that I could lean on him to provide spiritual support that was built on the foundation of God's Word. It was evident to me that God had placed him in my life intentionally and that he was *my* person.

God was still working on me and ultimately wanted me to let go of certain things and certain people. Still blinded in this area of my life and, quite honestly, a bit frustrated, God used my friend to help expose me to my reality. I treasured all aspects of this man of faith. It was so refreshing to have someone of the opposite sex who was also a man of God and someone with whom I could talk, laugh, and feel comfortable. He and I didn't have to drink, go clubbing, or partake in any unholy extracurricular activities to connect to each other. Our connection was built on our faith and desire to be obedient to God. After he met my son and I met his, he somehow naturally treated my boy the same way that he treated his own son, as did I with his son. It was a beautiful thing to witness.

In an era when fathers were receiving negative press, this man was doing and being what a father should do and be. He was the complete opposite of the stereotypical father that you generally see and hear about. I *loved* the way he cared for his son and how he stepped in and cared for my son in the same way. To think—before leaving my marriage I was concerned about my son not being raised by his father, and now, God had eased that worry by bringing more than one father figure into my son's life. You see how faithful God is?

Soon enough, me, Terry, and our boys all began hanging out together, and our quality time resembled the makings of a beautiful family. These family outings only heightened my already positive interest in him. We would spend hours and hours talking on the phone about everything and sometimes about absolutely nothing. The more we talked and hung out, the more I grew fond of him. He was a blessing to both me and my son.

Eventually, what had started off as a platonic friendship took a turn, and after both of our divorces were final, we decided to move out of the friend zone and begin dating. This transition was, however, private until we were ready to make it public knowledge. He and I both agreed that some things are better kept to ourselves until the right time. We felt that this would help keep others out of our business and aid us in not having to filter through so many different opinions that good ole' Baptist folks often freely give (even when you don't ask). By this time, our newly found connection was beginning to confidentially blossom.

Here we were in a flourishing relationship, each of us being given another chance at love. I will not pretend that everything was all peaches and cream between us. Like any relationship, we had our share of ups and downs, but in spite of the downs, we enjoyed and also supported each other in reaching our life goals.

We took our time learning about each other, which is something I wasn't used to, but it proved to be the best route. It ultimately continued even after our initial excitement had passed.

We had dated for six years when the day came that our relationship was made public. Terry's father, the late Dr. Cato Brooks Jr., revealed our secret relationship to a church full of people. Neither of us had a clue of what was about to take place. However, things happen for a reason, and to this day, I am so glad that he, from the pulpit, took the liberty of sharing with the congregation how much he appreciated me for loving his son as I did and how he enjoyed sharing my son with my parents as his grandson. He went on and on, and to our surprise, he even made me get up from the opposite side of the church and walk over to the other side of the church to sit with his family. I usually don't embarrass easily, but I was *extremely* embarrassed that day. Yet I love him even more for doing what God led him to do. Even after this big announcement, in true Terry and Monique fashion, our relationship continued to remain largely private. Only those closest to us had the inside scoop, but that announcement would serve as a sneak peek into our future life together.

Much time passed since that *wonderful* Sunday. While dating Terry, I finished my bachelor's degree and began working as a teacher. This career of working with students, teachers, and even parents led to many connections with people. Those connections grew into trust and people confiding in me with some of their deepest emotions.

I began to see God directing me toward another career path that would ultimately lead me further into his purpose for my life. With the help and encouragement of *my guy*, I enrolled in seminary for my master's degree in Christian counseling. Everything was on the up and up—school, home, and my relationship. All aspects of my life just seemed to improve even further after God placed Terry in it. Our love and respect for each other grew to the extent that we often had extensive discussions about marriage, and although the desire was evident, we took things slowly, not wanting to rush into marriage too soon. Neither of us wanted to run the risk of making the same mistakes we had made in our previous marriages. As a result, he and I both took our time and grew in our knowledge of marriage, its purpose, and our roles as husband and wife. When we were ready to say "I do," he chose the date and even took the initiative in getting the planning started. I mean, he really took the lead in the initial planning of our wedding, and that was okay with me; I wasn't really into all the little details anyway. All I really wanted was to be present before God and become his wife.

Though there was a fair amount of kinks to iron out before marriage, my love for him only grew stronger as we worked out each one. Before our big day, we had several conversations in which Terry helped me understand my role as *his* wife and how God created *him* to be my provider and protector and the head of our family. He also shared with me how significant it was for me, as his wife, to allow him to be my provider, protector, and leader. Knowing God's purpose for our lives, which was ultimately marriage, led us to actively work toward God's will together.

After years of premarital preparation, we were ready to finally fulfill God's ultimate purpose for our lives. We said "I do" for the last time on February 14, 2015. Yep, he chose Valentine's Day. Romantic, right? Well, that's my guy. The wedding was to be a big surprise to our attendees. We kept the day a secret the same way we had kept our dating a secret. (Of course, it was only right that we remained consistent.) The only information those outside of our circle had was what Terry's father had disclosed on that revealing Sunday. To engage our uninformed family and friends in our surprise nuptials, we told them they were going to be guest panelists at a Family Matters conference. They all came prepared with notepads and pens ready for a discussion on family, with no idea they were about to witness the vows Terry and I were going to pledge to each other before God. It was a great surprise and a sweet and memorable moment for all who were truly happy for us.

That day was perfect and one I'll never forget. God had given me another chance at love with a man he had handpicked just for me! Even through our friendship and dating, I could never imagine that I would be where I am today. Our marriage would be different than what we had both experienced before because *our* marriage would be based on purpose and not pleasure. My husband is amazing! He is an excellent protector and provider for our family. I'm grateful to God that he thought enough of me to bless me with a man who takes such great care of me and our boys. He's not perfect, but neither am I, and since God is okay with that, we both have no choice but to be okay with it too. We get it wrong sometimes, and we also get it right, but together we're constantly working toward a better marriage. God knew exactly what I needed, and he knew exactly what my son needed. Reflecting on the circumstances of when we first met, I actually believe that God was looking out for my son, and I just so happened to be a blessed bystander. There is no way that I can take credit for what God has done in my life, all despite my mess-ups. That's why the day of our marriage is so unforgettable—it was the beginning of a phenomenal *new* life for all four of us.

In all that I have experienced, I can confidently say that God has delivered me and I am better as a result. I was a complete mess in my younger days, but God turned my life around. Who knew that I, a mess of a Monique, would turn out to be a Certified Christian Counselor, mentor, and Certified Mental Health Coach married to the senior pastor of one of the most prominent and fastest-growing churches in San Diego. Oh yeah, did I mention that my husband is a pastor? Who would have ever guessed it? That's the sense of humor God has! My story is a testimony to all women that it doesn't matter who you are, where you're from, or what you've done. If you will only surrender your life to the Lord and allow him to take control, he can also turn your mess into a miracle!

Reflection

I must say that I loved this journey, not because I enjoyed the hurt and pain that came with it but because of the healing I've experienced and the assurance that my Savior is always near. I will never have to wonder again whether there will be another episode of having the inability to trace him. I am stronger now than I was before. My faith is greater than before. Since I realized that he is near when I call him, calling on him is the first option. The *truth* is what sets me free, and I will forever be honest during my time with him. After all, he already knows everything.

One thing I learned during this season is that I will forever need moments of solitude with God. The enemy is always lurking to see where he can cause chaos and confusion in our lives, and temptation will always be an issue that tries to separate us from God.

In 1 Corinthians 10:13 we read, "No temptation has overtaken you that is not common to man. God is faithful, and he will not let you be tempted beyond your ability, but with the temptation He will also provide the way of escape, that you may be able to endure it." Living a life with Jesus as my guide, I now understand this scripture more than ever. It doesn't matter where you look up and find yourself, there is always a way out. I encourage you not to keep going when you know that you have made a mistake. Get out as soon as you sense that you're headed in the wrong direction. God has already prepared your escape route—just pay attention. I am not suggesting that you betray anyone, but betraying God is worse than betraying humans because no person can free your life like God can. There is no *comforter*, there is no *redeemer*, and there is no *Savior* like the *One* sent to die on the cross and who rose in victory so that everyone could have the opportunity to live a victorious life. I can't imagine anything ever pushing me past temptation again and taking me back to betraying God and the love of my Savior, Jesus Christ.

Even today, if you were to ask me if I ever lived up to everything in that blueprint I laid out for myself earlier, I would be pleased to tell you that I didn't and there was a reason for that. Whether or not we acknowledge the reality of God's sovereignty, it is real. "We can make our plans, but the Lord determines our steps" (Proverbs 16:9). This verse says that God, himself, has a plan for my life and your life as well, and he will take the liberty to make sure his will happens.

It is not because I am so great, but because my God is great! He was there through all of my mess and turned it into a miracle. "And you know that for those who love God all things work together for good, for those who are called according to his purpose" (Romans 8:28). While you're in the thick of things, you can't fathom how they can work together for any kind of good. That is the greatness of God. It is not for you or me to figure out. This is how the Master works—you do your part and He will do His.

I had made a mess of my life and I knew it, but the way in which God brought me through my storms is nothing short of a miracle. I was thankful to God for my time of solitude that allowed me to reconnect with Him. I reflect on the apostle Paul, who had an issue that troubled him. He sought the Lord to remove it from him, but God answered, "My grace is sufficient for you, for my power is made perfect in weakness." Then in response, Paul says, "Therefore, I will boast all the more gladly of my weaknesses, so that the power of Christ may rest upon me" (2 Corinthians 12:9). Paul's dilemma helps me to understand that my situation may have been a complete mess, but God's strength came through like a mighty lion on my behalf. His grace covered me and has given me the courage I needed to seek peace, healing, forgiveness, restoration, and redemption.

No matter how many times I rehearse in my mind what happened in that chapter of my life and no matter how often I share with others in hopes that it will encourage and point them in the direction of Christ, it cannot repay my Savior, who is so great, so forgiving, so merciful, so gracious, and so faithful. There is nothing and no one, not even Monique, that could separate me from his love. No matter what I did and no matter how many bad decisions I made, God never ceased loving me.

Paul is a very good example of God's love being expressed no matter the situation. He appears again in Romans, saying, "For I am sure that neither death nor life, nor angels nor rulers, nor things present nor things to come, nor powers, nor height nor depth, nor anything else in all creation, will be able to separate us from the love of God in Christ Jesus our Lord" (Romans 8:38–39). I couldn't agree more with Paul. For God to call me into His presence after all that I had been through, mostly self-inflicted, I knew that no one could ever fix it or, rather, fix me but God. There are not enough words in all of human vocabulary to express how grateful I am for God's intervening power of change in my life.

Simply reflecting on that time in my life brings tears to my eyes. He never let go of me. If I could parallel my life with words that describe what I never want to be again, it would require a book of its own. I now understand that pride will separate you from God's will. "There is a way that seems right to a man, but its end is the way to death" (Proverbs 14:12). Just because it seems right doesn't mean it's right for you. God is never going to force anyone to do anything, yet there he stands with the perfect solution waiting for us to take notice of it. I took many twists and turns trying to feel better about what I had done, but there was nothing around the corner that was better than going through with God as my guide.

All I can do now is thank God for his healing and restorative power. I could not have come out had I not gone through. Without him, my story could not have turned out the way it did; and to think, God is not yet finished with me. The end of one episode was torturous, but my new beginning brings tears of joy!

If I could leave you with any final thoughts, they would be

to examine your life and think about the decisions you made to get where you are. If God is not at the center of your decisions, make it your business to make room for him because without him you can't live life to its full potential.

After reading about my roller-coaster of a life and now being exposed to your twists, turns, and loops, what can you do at this point in your life to seek healing, forgiveness, restoration, and redemption? How will you work toward being a better woman, daughter, mother, friend, and wife—but most of all a better child of God?

A Prayer for My Readers

Abba Father, thank you for writing my story so perfectly, for forgiving me, healing me, restoring me, reviving me, and redeeming me. Only you could turn my mess into a miracle! For each woman who made an investment in herself by reading my book, for the time and space you've given them to reflect and respond, but most importantly for the time they've spent with you, I thank you! Honor their efforts and hear their hearts cry out. When it's all said and done, allow them to experience your forgiveness, *self-forgiveness*, healing, restoration, and redemption.

In Jesus' name, Amen

About the Author

California native Monique Antoinette Brooks serves as a long-standing member and the first lady alongside her husband, Terry Wayne Brooks, senior pastor, at Bayview Church in San Diego, California.

An advocate for education, Monique earned a bachelor of arts degree in interdisciplinary studies with a concentration in prekindergarten through eighth grade from Western Governors University. She went on to utilize her degree in the field of education, where she worked as a before- and after-school program site director with the Lemon Grove School District for over nine years.

While working as a site director, Monique found herself to be a confidant as well as an emotional support system for students, parents, and many of her coworkers. This experience sparked a desire in Monique to further help individuals cope with the emotions and issues they face regarding their life circumstances through counseling. On God's terms, she further pursued her education and earned a master of arts degree in leadership ministry with a focus in Christian counseling from Faith International University and Seminary. Following her degree completion, Monique set out to fulfill her God-given purpose and developed a ministry within her church, built around educating and counseling individuals in the areas of mental health, marriage and family counseling, as well as addiction and recovery, with an emphasis on the faith-based perspective.

Monique is also a mental health advocate, Certified Mental Health Coach, and a Question, Persuade, and Refer Trainer for suicide prevention.

In addition to being a full-time Certified Christian Counselor, Monique wears many hats. She has served as the music ministry director of the youth and young adult choir ChoZen, the coordinator and facilitator for the single and parenting ministry, and a Bible teacher. She is currently a member of the Bayview worship team, a small-group facilitator, and director for the youth leadership development program #iChooseLife.

In addition to being very active in ministry, Monique constantly seeks spiritual growth through the Word of God and many other books she reads. Monique finds joy in not only serving God's people through various ministries but fulfilling her God-given role as a loving and attentive wife to her husband and a mother to their two sons, Jordan and Amarion.